*To our precious children—
Rob, Claire, Brittnye, and Ashley*

Photo Credits include: Cleo Photography–pages 11, 13 and 21; Mark Romine/TSI–page 31; David Stewart/TSI–page 35; Pascal Crapet/TSI–page 41; From *A Week in the Life of the LCMS*–page 43.

Scripture quotations marked NKJV are from New King James edition, copyright ©1979. Used by permission.

All other Scripture quotations are taken from the HOLY BIBLE, NEW INTERNATIONAL VERSION®. NIV®. Copyright © 1973, 1978, 1984 by International Bible Society. Used by permission of Zondervan Publishing House. All rights reserved.

Copyright © 1999 Concordia Publishing House
3558 S. Jefferson Avenue, St. Louis, MO 63118-3968

Manufactured in China

All rights reserved. No part of this publication may be reproduced, stored in a retrieval system, or transmitted, in any form or by any means, electronic, mechanical, photocopying, recording, or otherwise, without the prior written permission of Concordia Publishing House.

1 2 3 4 5 6 7 8 9 10   08 07 06 05 04 03 02 01 00 99

The  of CHRISTIAN MARRIAGE

Twenty-six ways to love and nurture
your spouse today and every day

Robert & Debra Bruce

Acknowledge

your similarities and celebrate your differences. Be yourself in the marriage, and allow your spouse to do the same.

Nevertheless, each one should retain the place in life that the Lord assigned to him and to which God has called him. This is the rule I lay down in all the churches.
1 Corinthians 7.17

Brighten
your spouse's day
with a good morning kiss,
no matter what the problems were
the day before, and thank God for
sending this person into your life.

Greet one another with a holy kiss.
Romans 16.16

Call

upon the reservoirs of peace,
strength, and assurance that are
available to you through Christ.
When your world is caving
in around you, join together
and reach out to an unshakable
source of strength—
Christ Himself.

And the peace of God, which transcends
all understanding, will guard your hearts
and your minds in Christ Jesus.

Philippians 4:7

Develop

a best friendship
with your spouse by keeping
an open mind and a willing heart.
Discover your inner strengths, and
hold strong to the truth that God
will care for all your needs.

Two are better than one, because they
have a good return for their work.
Ecclesiastes 4:9

Encourage
your spouse to become
all God intended by lifting up
special talents and attributes and
affirming the "little" things he or
she does. Relationships die of
neglect, so stay alert!

How fair is your love, my sister,
my spouse! How much better than wine
is your love, and the scent of your
perfume than all spices!
Song of Solomon 4:10 (NKJV)

Focus

on how God's love is revealed to you through your spouse each day—a gentle touch, an unexpected phone call to say "I love you," or a tender glance across the table. Thank God for these reminders of unconditional love.

Pleasant words are a honeycomb,
sweet to the soul and healing to the bones.
Proverbs 16:24

Give

to your spouse
without any strings attached
—just because—
and experience a
stronger emotional bond.

Remembering the words the Lord Jesus Himself said: "It is more blessed to give than to receive."

Acts 20:35

Honor

your marriage covenant
even if you don't feel loving
at the moment. Best friendships
in marriage depend on active love
with the realization that you are
one soul sharing two
different bodies.

Finally, all of you, live in harmony with one another; be sympathetic, love as brothers, be compassionate and humble.
1 Peter 3:8

Identify
stumbling blocks
in your relationship.
Openly discuss how to turn
these into stepping stones
to experience growth and
increased intimacy.

Be kind and compassionate
to one another, forgiving each other,
just as in Christ God forgave you.
Ephesians 4:32

Join
together and share
the mundane responsibilities
of life—housekeeping, yard work,
and paying bills—so that one
person is not constantly having
to deal with these each day.

Carry each other's burdens, and in this
way you will fulfill the law of Christ.
Galatians 6:2

Keep

prayer lists and talk openly about God's answers to prayers. Remember, God can say "yes," "no," "maybe," or "I'm going to surprise you."

My God will meet all your needs.
Philippians 4:19

Listen

to God speak during quiet times together. Read Scriptures, join hands in prayer, and become aware of God's presence in your lives through contemplative listening.

If two of you on earth agree about anything you ask for, it will be done for you by My Father in heaven.

Matthew 18:19

Make

the decision to turn over
a new leaf, forgiving and forgetting
past hurts and striving toward
emotional connectedness.

Offer hospitality to one another
without grumbling.

1 Peter 4:9

Nurture

intimacy in your marriage
by making it a priority over
career, kids, and commitments.
Set aside time each day to spend
together, and also make time
once a week to go out—alone.

Marriage should be honored by all.
Hebrews 13:4

Open
your hearts
to spiritual experiences,
which can emerge from the most
unexpected places—gardening,
playing tennis, watching your
children interact, or
praying together.

Where the Spirit of the Lord is,
there is freedom.
2 Corinthians 3:17

Plan

a ritual for you and your spouse that includes together time— having coffee together each morning, listening to favorite music, going on an after-dinner walk. Rituals can increase intimacy and trust, especially if they are something you both look forward to regularly.

Always try to be kind to each other and to everyone else.

1 Thessalonians 5:15

Quit

allowing destructive habits
and negative emotional behaviors
to injure your relationship.
Never allow yourself to get
too harried, angry, bored,
stressed, or tired.

Live in peace with each other.
1 Thessalonians 5:13

Renew

your commitment to Christ together, and remember that with God in Christ at the hub of your relationship, all things become possible.

For this reason a man will leave his father and mother and be united to his wife, and the two will become one flesh. This is a profound mystery—but I am talking about Christ and the church. However, each one of you, also must love his wife as he loves himself, and the wife must respect her husband.

Ephesians 5:31–33

Spend

time alone for spiritual recovery and enjoy personal renewal. Get your priorities in order and let go of commitments that are overburdening.

Teach me Your way, O LORD;
lead me in a straight path.

Psalm 27:11

Take

a strong stand on issues
that are important to you, and
respect your spouse's opinions,
even if they are different.

Love … bears all things,
believes all things, hopes all things,
endures all things.
                1 Corinthians 13:4,7 (NKJV)

Use
a spiritual journal
to write down your daily
experiences, then share these with
your spouse. Look over this journal
in a few weeks to see how God
brought you through life's
ebb and flow.

To everything there is a season,
a time for every purpose under heaven.
Ecclesiastes 3:1 (NKJV)

Verbalize

your feelings when you
are alone with your spouse.
Avoid letting anger, jealousy,
or hostility build up inside, and
learn how to talk about feelings
without hurting each other.

Pride only breeds quarrels, but wisdom
is found in those who take advice.

Proverbs 13:10

Worship

regularly in Christ's church,
and shift your burdens from
your own shoulders to God's.
Find strength in the Word and
the people of the Lord.

I can do everything through Him who gives me strength.

Philippians 4:13

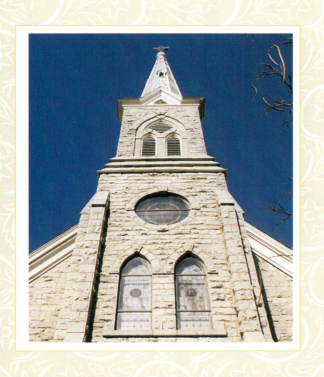

eXamine

how your spouse perceives you. Listen to what you say to your spouse, and watch how you act and react. Use this observational process to make much-needed changes in your relationship.

Therefore, as God's chosen people, holy and dearly loved, clothe yourselves with compassion, kindness, humility, gentleness and patience. Bear with each other and forgive whatever grievances you may have against one another.
Colossians 3:12–14

Yield

to God the stresses
and hardships life tosses at you,
and know that God's strength can
see you through the toughest
of times.

Praise be to the God and Father of
our Lord Jesus Christ, the Father of
compassion and the God of all comfort,
who comforts us in all our troubles.
2 Corinthians 1:3–4

Zealously
anticipate new beginnings
each day as you travel side by side
on the journey of life.
Let God's abiding love
be the spark that refreshes and
energizes your travels together.

May the God of peace … equip you with everything good for doing His will.
Hebrews 13:20–21

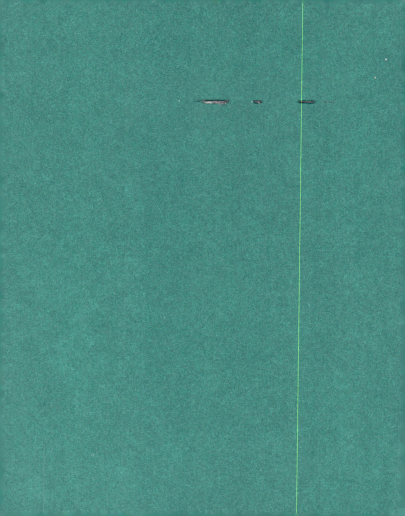